Today I Feel Happy

Written and illustrated by
Monica Timmel

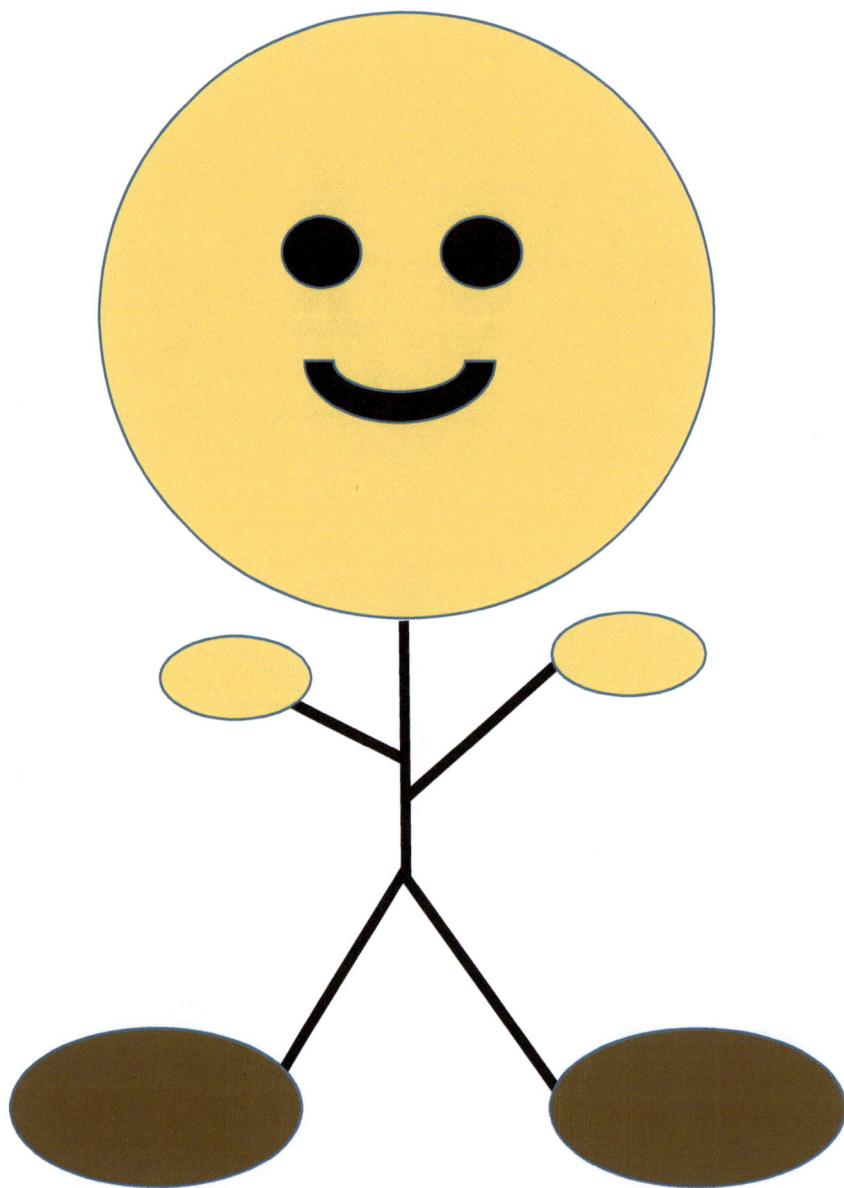

Today I feel happy!
My smile says it all.

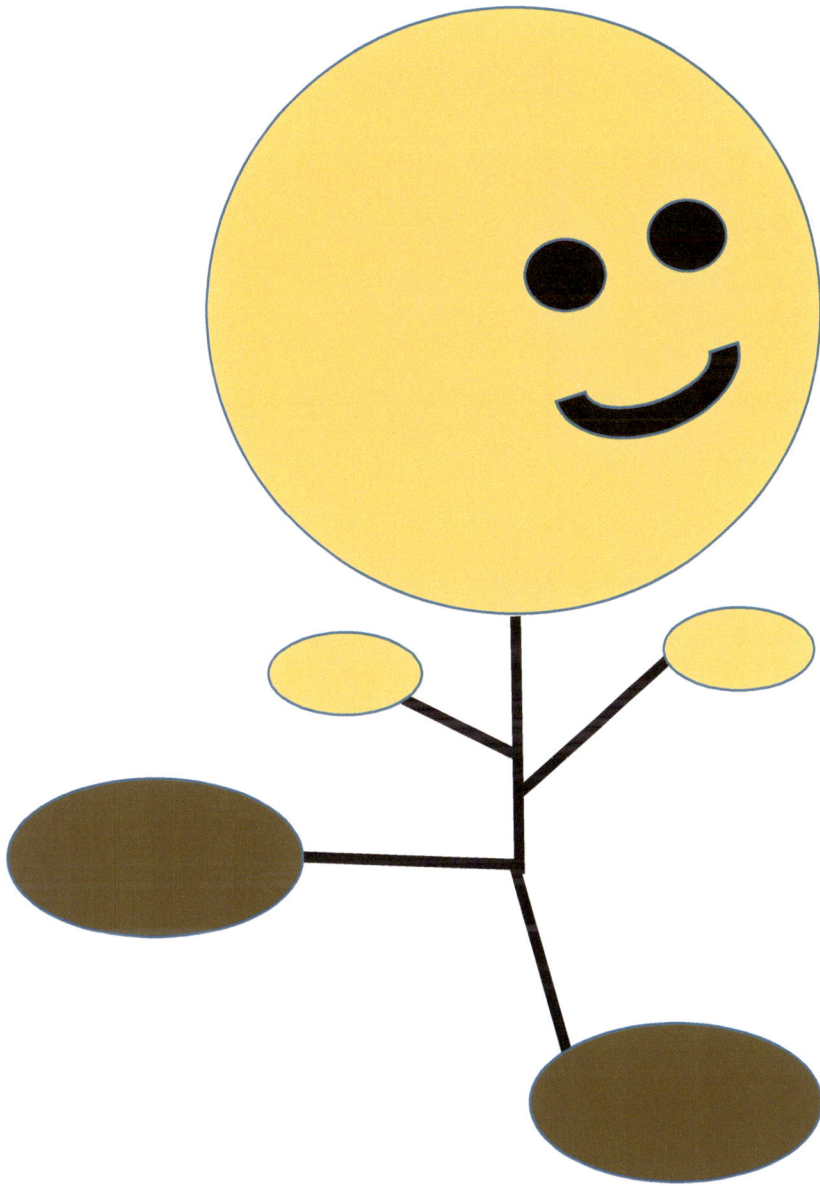

I'm skipping and jumping,
just having a ball!

I wake up to the sunshine,
eat bacon and eggs.

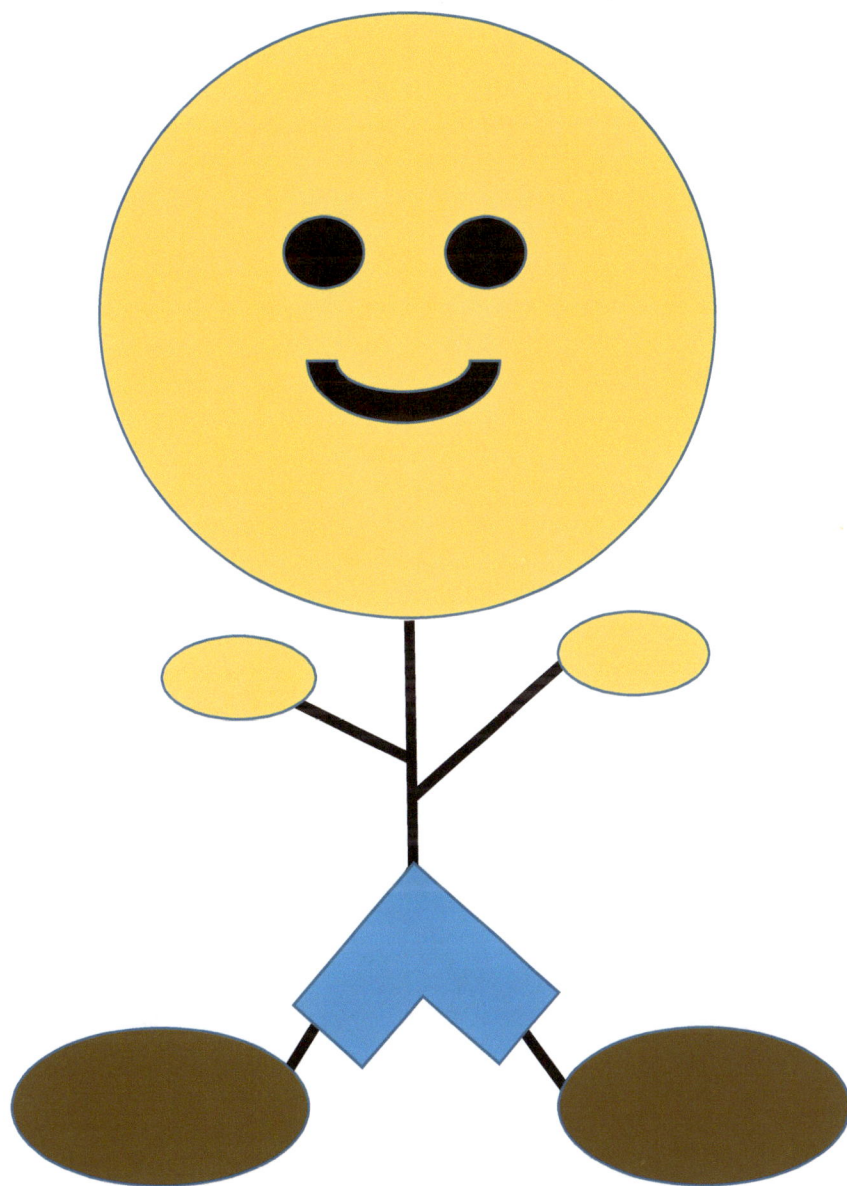

Mom says I can wear
my new shorts on my legs.

On the bus I am able
to sit by my friend.

We laugh and share stories,
it's fun to pretend!

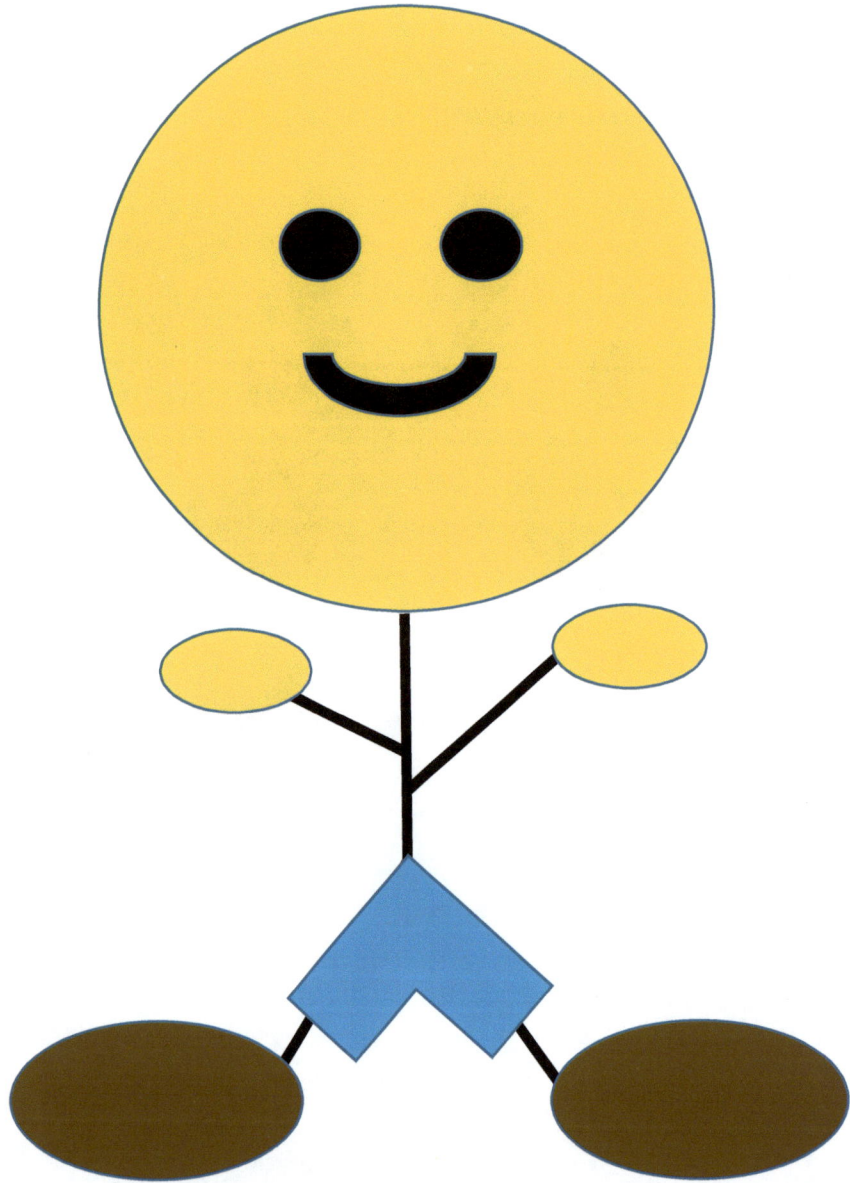

When I walk in my classroom
my teacher tells me,

it is my turn to care for our pet, Broccoli!

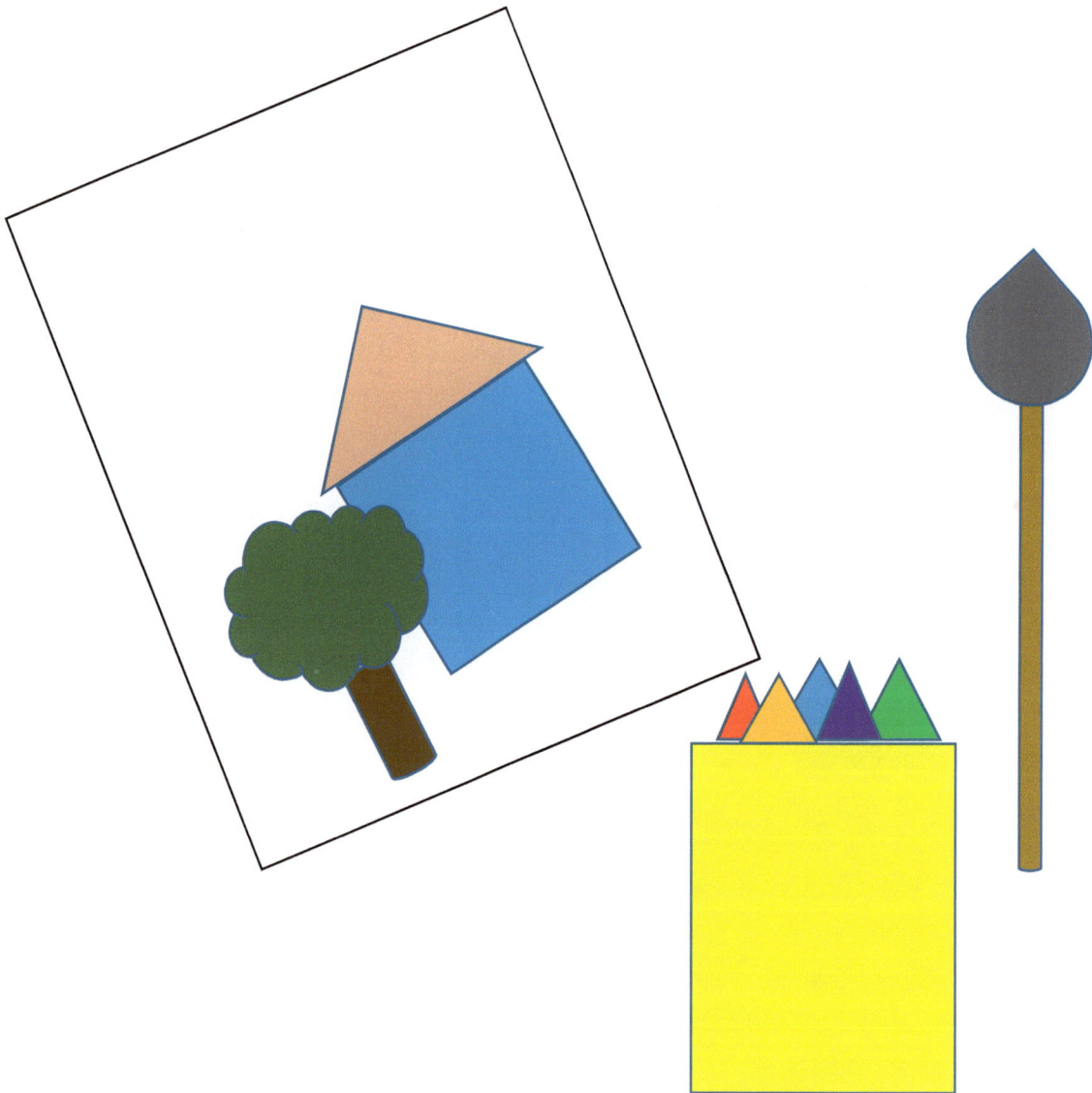

My class gets to paint,
and color, and draw.

I make a tiger
with a polka-dot claw.

In gym class we play
with the huge parachute.

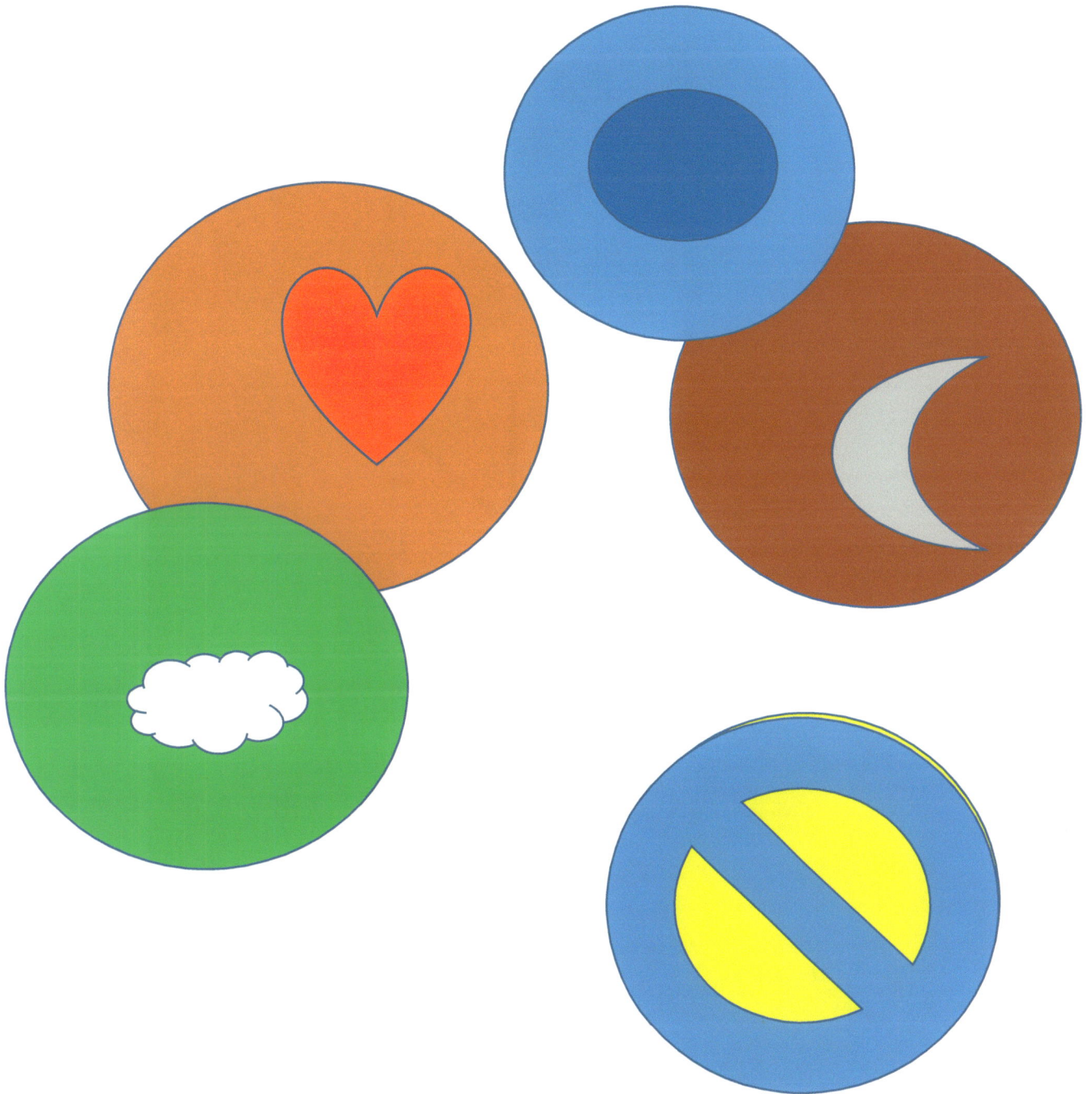

Launching balls in the air
is a laugh and a hoot!

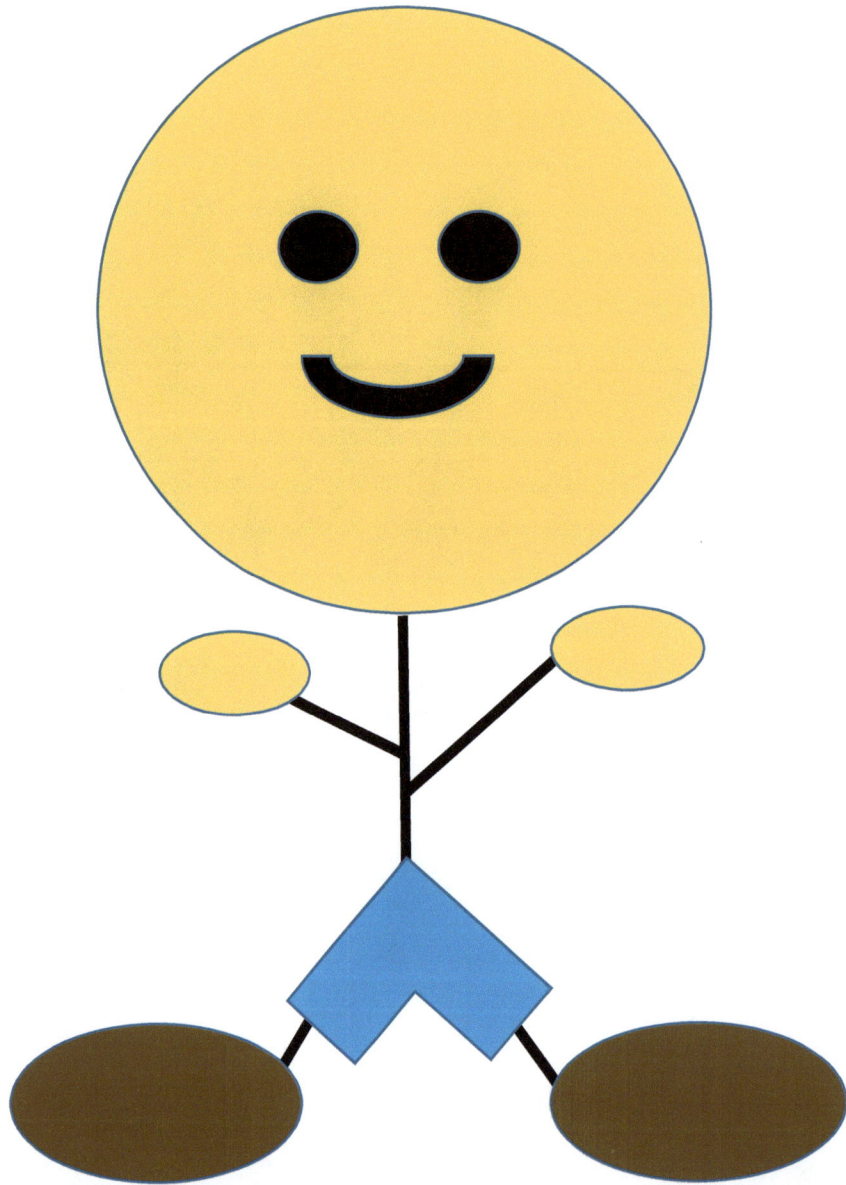

With a smile on my face
I walk happily along,

humming, and whistling,
and singing a song.

To the playground we go.
We run, hang, and swing.

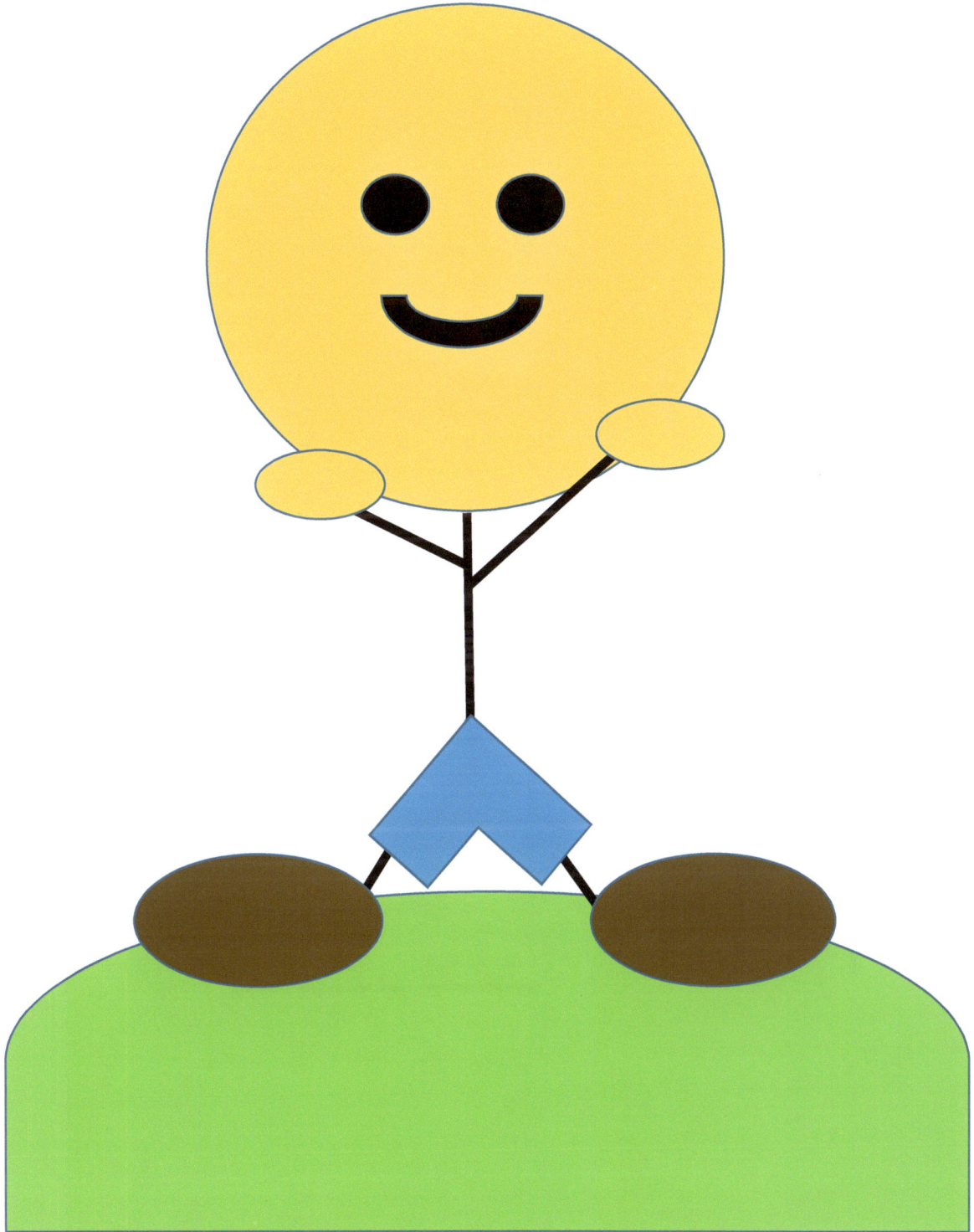

Football, tag, monkey bars,
"Look, I'm the King!"

Name _____

5-2= _____

3-2= _____

1-1= _____

In math we subtract,
it is really quite fun.

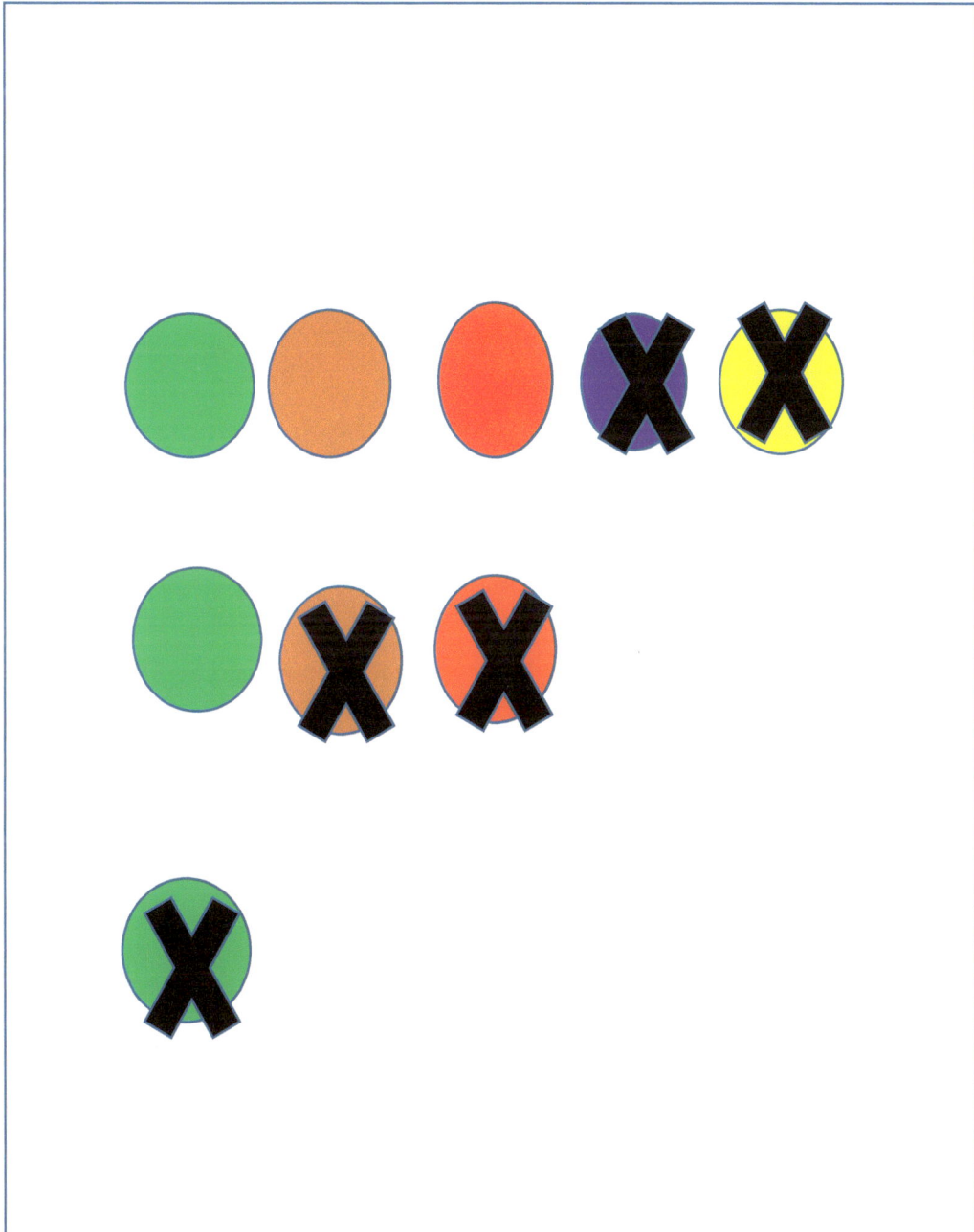

"Take away from the whole
until there is none."

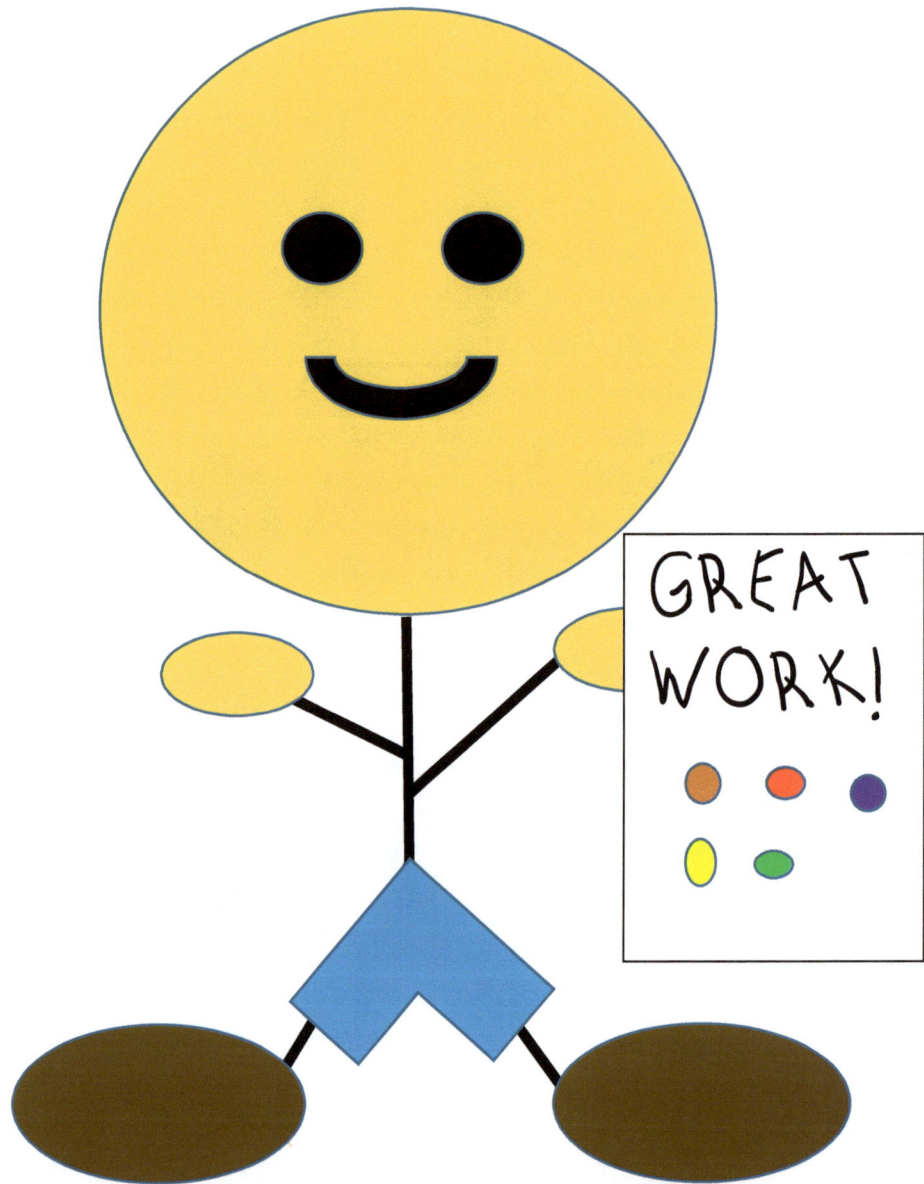

A smile <u>still</u> on my face
a "GREAT WORK!" in my hand,

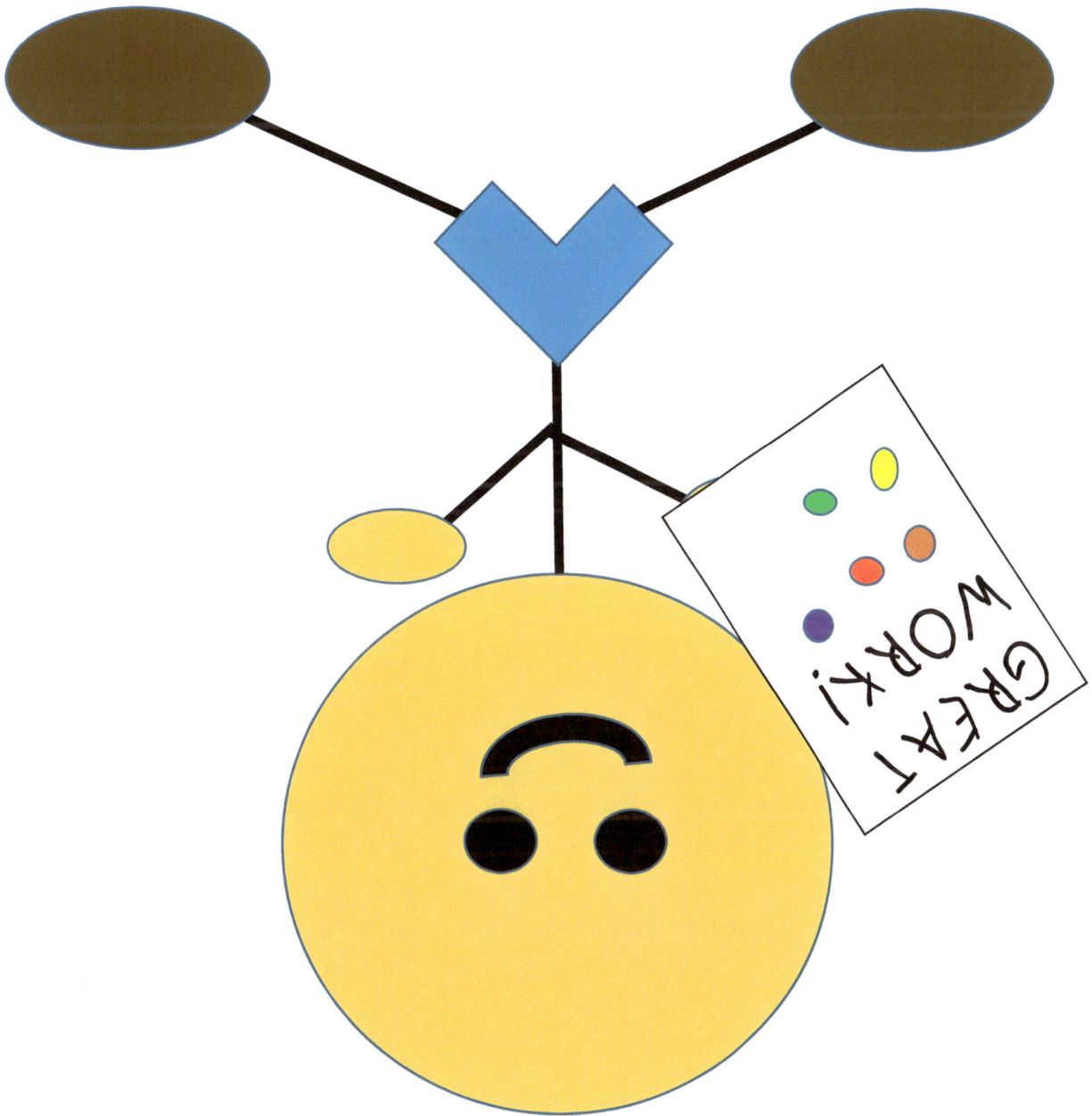

on the way home
I cartwheel and hand stand.

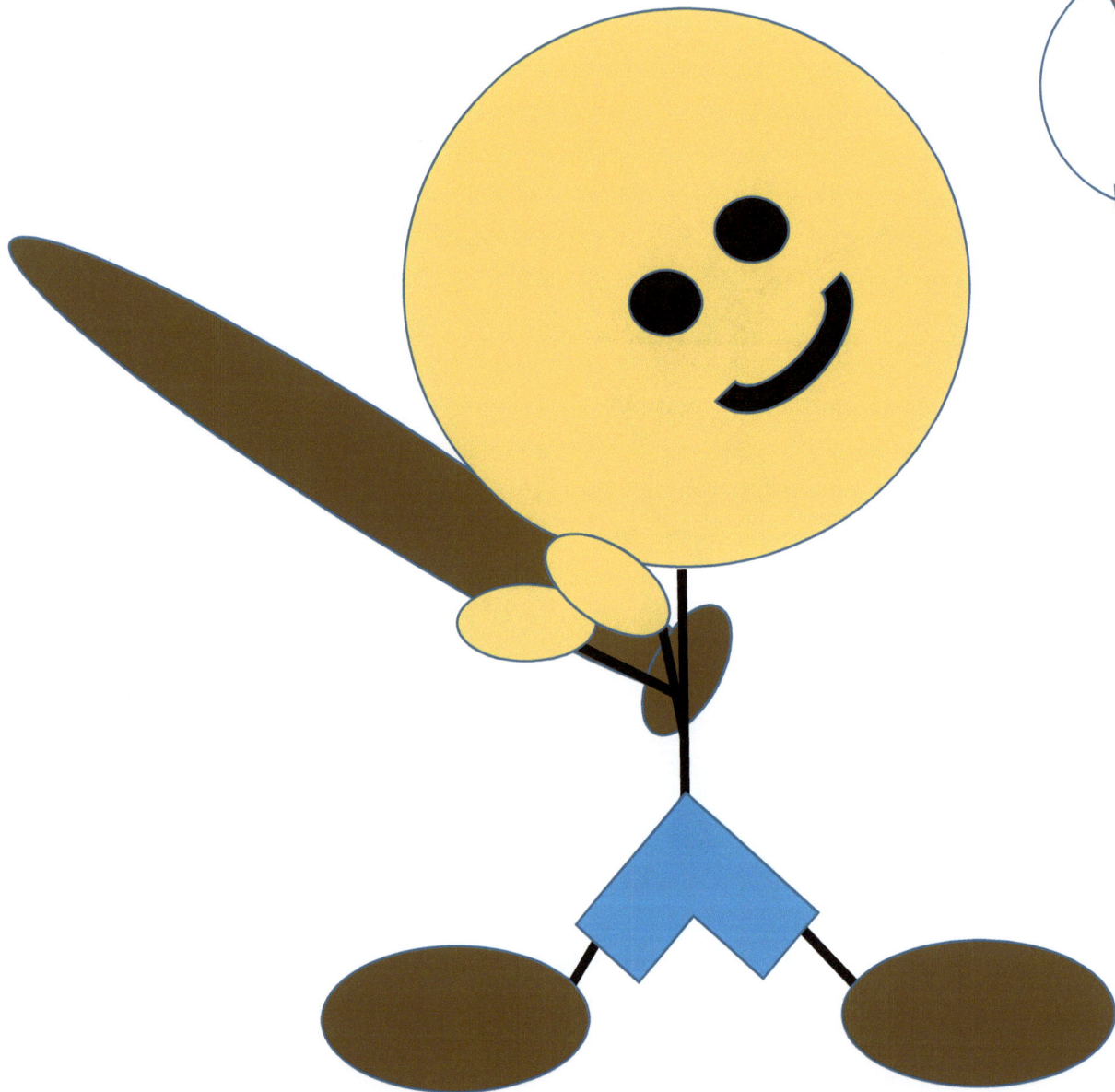

I play with my friends,
then it's time for homework,

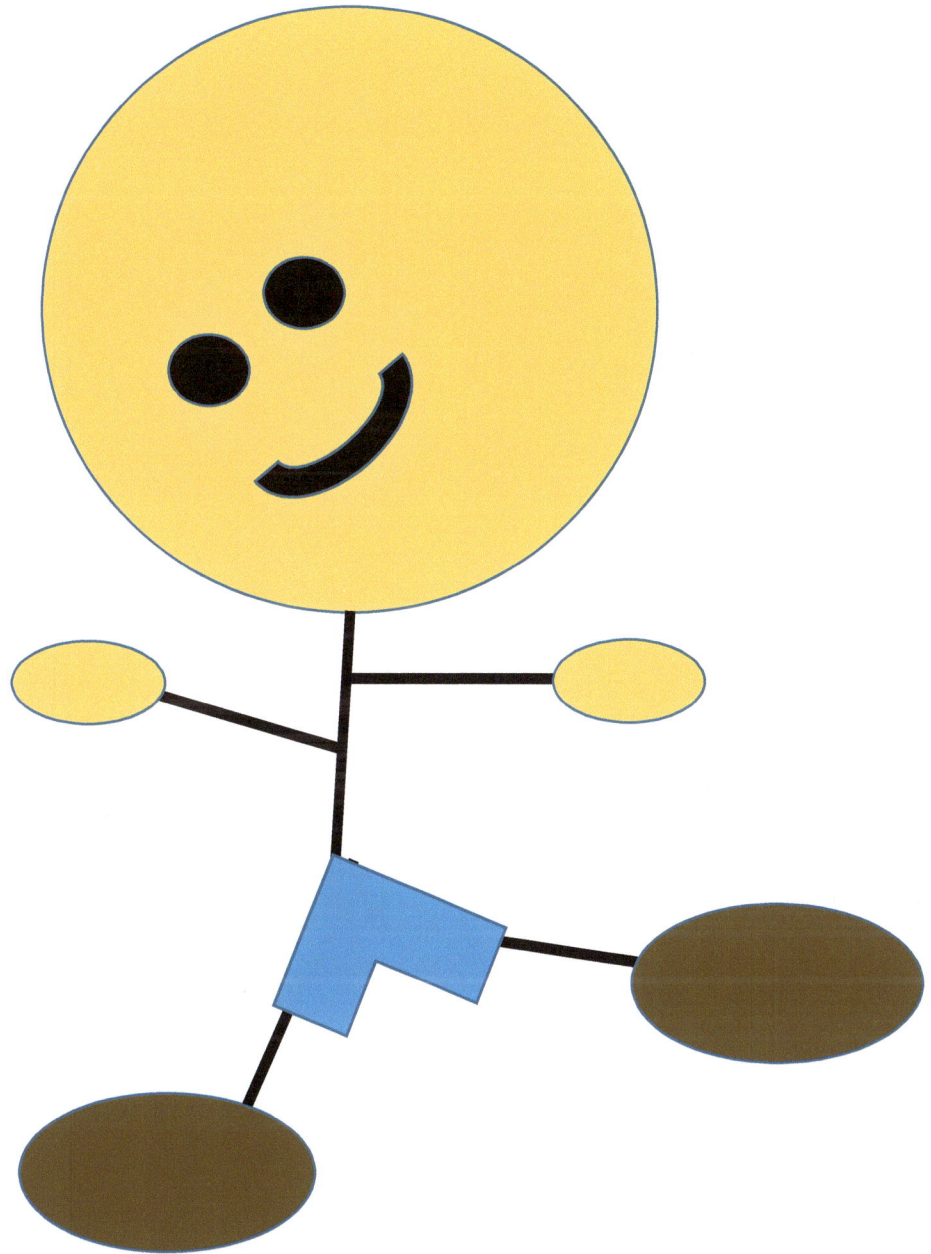

then a dance party,
LET'S GO BERSERK!!

A short bedtime story,
then my dreams I do see.

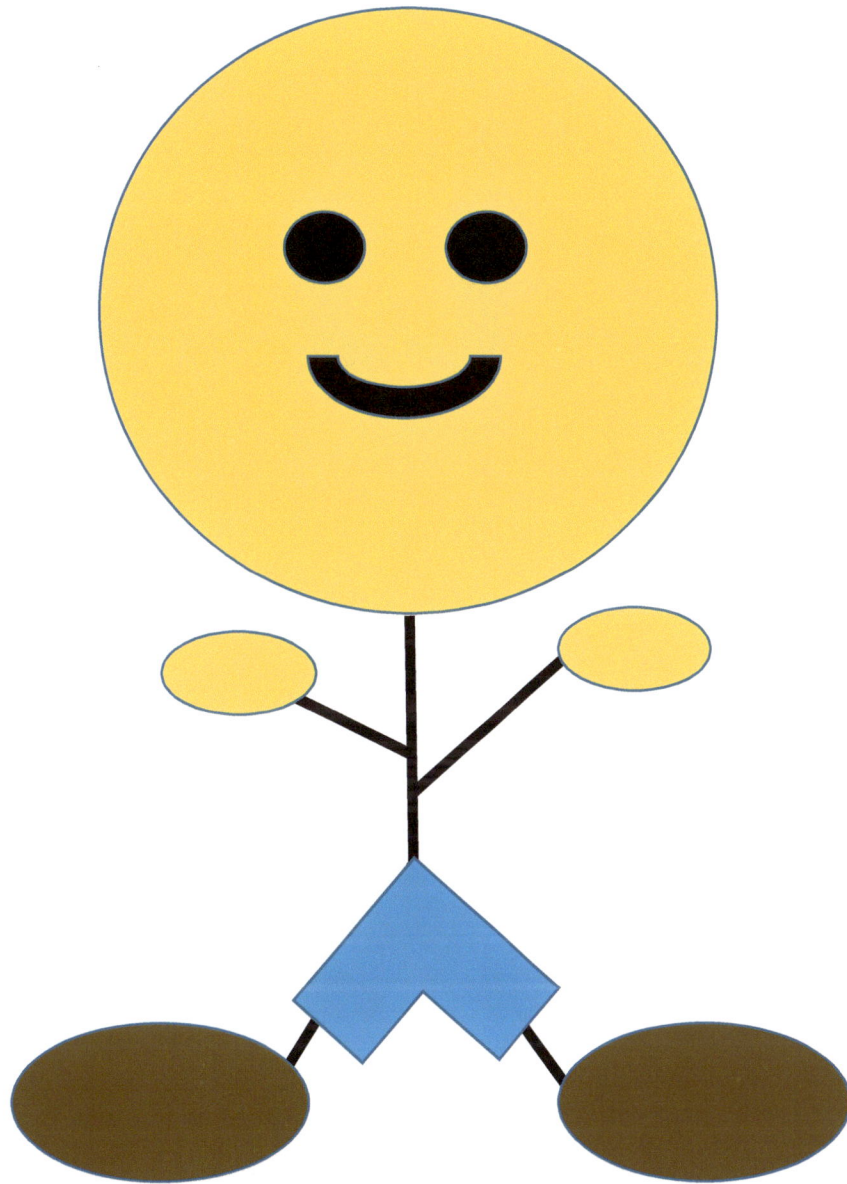

Today was a great day!
Today I felt happy!

Name _____

Draw a picture of when you feel happy.

Name _____

What animal do you like to draw?

Name _____

What do you look like doing a silly dance?

Name _____

Draw a picture of when you feel happy.

I feel happy when _____
_____
_____ .

Name _____

What animal do you like to draw?

I like to draw _____.

Name _____

What do you like to pretend?

www.ingramcontent.com/pod-product-compliance
Lightning Source LLC
Chambersburg PA
CBHW041223040426

42443CB00002B/66